Primary Source
125 Walnut Street
Watertown, MA 02472-4052
tel. 617-923-9933
info@primarysource.org
www.primarysource.org

World War II: On the Homefront

Edited by Phyllis Raybin Emert

Discovery Enterprises, Ltd.
Carlisle, Massachusetts

© Discovery Enterprises, Ltd., Carlisle, MA 01741

ISBN 1-878668-60-9 paperback edition
Library of Congress Catalog Card Number 96-84759

10   9   8   7   6   5   4   3   2   1

Printed in the United States of America

Subject Reference Guide:

WORLD WAR II: On the Homefront
edited by Phyllis Raybin Emert

World War II - Homefront — U.S. History

Japanese Internment — U.S. History

Women in the Workplace — U.S. History

Photos/Illustrations:

Front cover, top row: Courtesy of the Library of Congress.
Front cover, bottom row: The National Archives.

Dedication:

For Ross Farrin Goldman

Table of Contents

Foreword

The global conflict known as World War II involved every major power on earth and by the time it ended, more than thirty million people had lost their lives. Although nearly half a million Americans died in the war, the United States was the only major power to emerge from the conflict virtually unscathed and stronger than before.

The war touched the lives of all Americans and brought about immense changes in the social and economic structure of the society. This book attempts to show readers what life was like on the home front during the Second World War and how and why these changes took place.

Excerpts from radio broadcasts, presidential speeches, newspaper articles, magazine advertisements, posters, and the actual words of those who lived through those turbulent times will give the readers of today a glimpse into understanding past events and how they influence our lives today.

One thing is certain, after World War II, for better or for worse, life in America was never quite the same again.

Remember Pearl Harbor!

by
Phyllis Rabin Emert

By the early 1940s America was gradually coming out of the world-wide economic crisis known as the Great Depression which lasted throughout the decade of the 1930s. The widespread poverty and unemployment of the Depression helped in part to create the climate which nurtured the rise to power of the totalitarian and militaristic regimes of Germany, Japan, and Italy.

By December of 1941, Adolph Hitler's dreams of a New World Order and Japanese plans for an empire had plunged much of the world into war. Germany had easily conquered most of Europe and only Great Britain and the Soviet Union stood alone against the Nazi war machine. Meanwhile in the Pacific, the Japanese had invaded Manchuria and occupied much of China.

Many Americans were opposed to entering the War in late 1941 and preferred not to get involved in solving the problems of other countries. Although most supported the Lend-Lease Act in which war supplies were transferred to Great Britain and Russia, they wanted to stay out of the dispute and concentrate on solving the domestic problems of their own nation.

Sunday morning December 7, 1941 began in an ordinary way. While kids read about the adventures of Popeye and Flash Gordon in the comics, adults perused several stories on the front page about Japan. One story noted that the Japanese fleet was on the move in Southeast Asia. Another mentioned that negotiations were continuing in Washington with Japanese representatives to maintain peace in the Pacific. For many Americans, Japan was a faraway place, a tiny island nation which presented little or no threat to the power and might of the United States.

Before the day ended, Japanese carrier-based aircraft had attacked the U.S. Pacific Fleet at Pearl Harbor in Hawaii, sinking or severely damaging 19 naval vessels including eight battleships. 188 U.S. airplanes were destroyed, 2,280 servicemen were killed, 1,109 were wounded, and 68 civilians were killed. The following excerpts focus on the Japanese attack and its aftermath in the United States.

Reaction to Pearl Harbor

"We interrupt this program to bring you a special news bulletin. The Japanese have attacked Pearl Harbor...."

— John Daly, CBS Radio
December 7, 1941

❖ ❖ ❖ ❖ ❖ ❖

(Source: *1941-The Call to Battle Stations*, edited by Samuel I. Rosenman, New York: Harper & Brothers Publishers, 1950, page 514)

Yesterday, December 7, 1941 — a date which will live in infamy — the United States of America was suddenly and deliberately attacked by naval and air forces of the Empire of Japan.

The United States was at peace with that Nation and, at the solicitation of Japan, was still in conversation with its Government and its Emperor looking toward the maintenance of peace in the Pacific...

It will be recorded that the distance of Hawaii from Japan makes it obvious that the attack was deliberately planned many days or even weeks ago. During the intervening time the Japanese Government has deliberately sought to deceive the United States by false statements and expressions of hope for continued peace...

Yesterday the Japanese Government also launched an attack against Malaya.

Last night Japanese forces attacked Hong Kong.

Last night Japanese forces attacked Guam.

Last night Japanese forces attacked the Philippine Islands.

Last night the Japanese attacked Wake Island.

And this morning the Japanese attacked Midway Island...

No matter how long it may take us to overcome this premeditated invasion, the American people in their righteous might will win through to absolute victory.

I believe that I interpret the will of the Congress and of the people when I assert that we will not only defend ourselves to the uttermost but will make it very certain that this form of treachery shall never again endanger us...

With confidence in our armed forces — and with the unbounding determination of our people — we will gain the inevitable triumph — so help us God.

I ask that the Congress declare that since the unprovoked and dastardly attack by Japan on Sunday, December 7, 1941, a state of war has existed between the United States and the Japanese empire.

> — Franklin D. Roosevelt
> President of the United States
> Address to Congress, December 8, 1941

❖ ❖ ❖ ❖ ❖ ❖

Army information sources confirmed today that two squadrons of enemy planes — numbering about fifteen planes to a squadron — crossed the coastline west of San Jose Monday night and reconnoitered the San Francisco Bay area and other sections of California.

The Army said the presence of these squadrons of planes indicated in all probability that an enemy aircraft carrier was lurking off the coast, possibly as far out as 500 or 600 miles.

— *Associated Press*
December 8, 1941

❖ ❖ ❖ ❖ ❖ ❖

Hostile Planes Sighted At San Francisco
Alarm is Widespread

Two formations of "many planes," described as undoubtedly enemy aircraft, flew over the San Francisco Bay area tonight, it was announced...

Conflicting reports spread, contributing to the "war of nerves" as the sirens wailed and broadcasting was silenced.

— Lawrence E. Davies
The New York Times
December 9, 1941

❖ ❖ ❖ ❖ ❖ ❖

Common sense is thrown to the winds and any absurdity is believed.

— General Joseph Stilwell
Western Defense Command Headquarters
December, 1941

❖ ❖ ❖ ❖ ❖ ❖

On the morning of December eleventh, the Government of Germany, pursuing its course of world conquest, declared war against the United States.

The long known and the long expected has thus taken place. The forces endeavoring to enslave the entire world now are moving toward this hemisphere.

Never before has there been a greater challenge to life, liberty, and civilization.

Delay invites greater danger. Rapid and united effort by all of the peoples of the world who are determined to remain free will insure a world victory of the forces of justice and of righteousness over the forces of savagery and of barbarism.

Italy also has declared war against the United States.

I therefore request the Congress to recognize a state of war between the United States and Germany, and between the United States and Italy.

— Franklin D. Roosevelt
President of the United States
Message to Congress, December 11, 1941

❖ ❖ ❖ ❖ ❖ ❖

It is a war of purification in which the forces of Christian peace and freedom and justice and decency and morality are arrayed against the evil pagan forces of strife, injustice, treachery, immorality and slavery.

— Congressman John W. Flannagan Jr.
Democrat, Virginia, December, 1941

❖ ❖ ❖ ❖ ❖ ❖

(Source: *The Home Front - America During World War II*, by Mark Jonathan Harris, Franklin D. Mitchell and Steven J. Schechter, New York: G.P. Putnam's Sons, 1984, page 23)

...I turned on the radio about one-thirty in the afternoon, just as Mother called us to come to the dining room to have dinner.

I got so excited when the announcer broke through that we delayed our dinner for half an hour. We ate in a state of shock... I didn't expect Pearl Harbor. When it came, it was a tremendous shock.

I knew that this was a turning point, that our lives would never be the same again.

— Edward Osberg

❖ ❖ ❖ ❖ ❖ ❖

(Source: Harris, Mitchell, Schechter, *ibid.*, page 26)

The day of Pearl Harbor my wife and I were away for a Sunday trip, about forty miles from our home in Flint, Michigan. There was an immediate concern — uncertainty, panic, a feeling that you needed somehow to seek a place where you'd be protected. We got in our car and quickly started that forty-mile trip back home, knowing that was the best thing to do, to get home where you felt safe, where you'd have proper communications. I remember our feelings on the trip back. First it was indignation, then it turned to anger, and by the time one went to work the following morning it was determination: "They can't do that to us."

— Don Johnson

Changing to a Wartime Economy

by
Phyllis Raybin Emert

With the United States' entrance into the war, Americans united in the largest production increase in the country's economic history. Unemployment and any remaining traces of the Great Depression virtually disappeared as the nation geared up for wartime.

As millions of able-bodied men went into military service, new sources of workers entered the job force. Suddenly, industry began to recruit women, blacks, older workers, teenagers, migrant workers, and even the physically handicapped to fill the void left by servicemen now fighting overseas.

President Franklin Roosevelt used his frequent radio addresses to the nation (called Fireside Chats) to ask all Americans to join in the massive effort to win the war by "outproducing and overwhelming the enemy." And that's exactly what the people did. Almost overnight, the American economy converted to wartime production. Before long, major corporations were rolling out weapons of war instead of the usual consumer goods.

Roosevelt established the War Production Board (WPB) and appointed Donald M. Nelson as its head. Nelson immediately banned the production of nonessential items to the war effort, including new automobiles, refrigerators, and bicycles among others.

The Ford Motor Company began turning out B-24 Liberator bombers instead of cars and by 1944, the plant produced one every sixty-three minutes. General Motors assembled fighter planes and bomber parts instead of Buicks. Chrysler manufactured bomber fuselages. Aircraft companies such as Boeing, Douglas, and Bell expanded and enlarged existing facilities or built new ones.

Henry Kaiser changed the basics of shipbuilding by prefabricating sections of each new ship and then welding these sections together. His seven shipyards throughout the country were able to construct and launch a ship in less than 81 hours. Kaiser shipping accounted for one third of America's total ship production during World War II.

This immediate conversion to war production involved companies of all sizes and types. A soft-drink manufacturer loaded shell casings with explosives. A toy company made compasses. A company that manufactured typewriters now produced rifles. A piano factory produced airplane motors. A pinball machine maker manufactured armor-piercing shells. Instead of silk ribbons, one manufacturer built silk parachutes.

Plentiful jobs and new factories throughout the nation encouraged millions of Americans to leave their homes and move where they could find steady work and a good income. The Census Bureau estimated that during the war years, more than 15 million Americans changed residences. They headed far west to the airplane and shipbuilding plants of California, Oregon, and Washington. They traveled to manufacturing plants in the mid-West and factories in Virginia, Alabama, Maryland, and Florida.

With this migration of millions came sudden and unaccustomed growth and a severe housing shortage. Tent settlements and trailer camps sprang up everywhere and some landlords near large manufacturing plants rented beds to workers according to their shifts at the factories. In certain areas, like Willow Run, Michigan, site of the new Ford aircraft plant, temporary housing units were constructed for thousands of people.

By the time the war ended in 1945, the United States had produced more than twice as many goods as Germany, Italy and Japan combined. American industry had turned out an incredible total of nearly 300,000 airplanes, more than 70,000 ships and landing craft, over 86,000 tanks, and over 2 million military trucks, not to mention millions of rifles and machine guns, and tons of bombs and ammunition.

It's easy to understand why the Russian Premier Josef Stalin made the following toast at the Teheran Conference in 1943. Holding his glass high, Stalin faced President Roosevelt and said, "...to American production, without which this war would have been lost."

The following excerpts focus on all aspects of America's changeover to a wartime economy.

A Call to Service

(Source: Rosenman, *op. cit.*, pages 523-524, 526-528; *1942 - Humanity on the Defensive*, pages 36-38)

...We are now in this war. We are all in it - all the way. Every single man, woman, and child is a partner in the most tremendous undertaking of our American history...

It will not only be a long war, it will be a hard war. That is the basis on which we now lay all our plans. That is the yardstick by which we measure what we shall need and demand; money, materials, doubled and quadrupled production — ever-increasing. The production must be not only for our own Army and Navy and Air Forces. It must reinforce the other armies and navies and air forces fighting the Nazis and the war lords of Japan throughout the Americas and throughout the world...

The United States does not consider it a sacrifice to do all one can, to give one's best to our Nation, when the Nation is fighting for its existence and its future life.

It is not a sacrifice for any man, old or young, to be in the Army or the Navy of the United States. Rather is it a privilege.

It is not a sacrifice for the industrialist or the wage earner, the farmer or the shopkeeper, the trainman or the doctor, to pay more taxes, to buy more bonds, to forego extra profits, to work longer or harder at the task for which he is best fitted. Rather is it a privilege.

It is not a sacrifice to do without many things to which we are accustomed if the national defense calls for doing without...

There will be a clear and definite shortage of metals of many kinds for civilian use, for the very good reason that in our increased program we shall need for war purposes more than half of that portion of the principal metals which during the past year have gone into articles for civilian use. Yes, we shall have to give up many things entirely...

— President Franklin D. Roosevelt
Fireside Chat, December 9, 1941

❖ ❖ ❖ ❖ ❖ ❖

This production of ours in the United States must be raised far above present levels, even though it will mean the dislocation of the lives and occupations of millions of our own people. We must raise our sights all along the production line. Let no man say it cannot be done. It must be done — and we have undertaken to do it...

Production for war is based on men and women — the human hands and brains which collectively we call Labor. Our workers stand ready to work long hours; to turn out more in a day's work; to keep the wheels turning and the fires burning twenty-four hours a day, and seven days a week...

War costs money...It means cutting luxuries and other non-essentials. In a word, it means an "all-out" war by individual effort and family effort in a united country...

— President Franklin D. Roosevelt
Address on the State of the Union
January 1942

Production of Selected Munitions Items

July 1, 1940 - July 31, 1945

(Source: Rosenman, *Humanity on the Defense, op. cit.,* page 61)

Item	July 1, 1940 through December 1941	1942	1943	1944	Jan. 1, 1945 through July 31, 1945	Cumulative July 1, 1940 through July 31, 1945
Military airplanes & special purpose aircraft	23,228	47,859	85,930	96,359	43,225	**296,601**
Naval ships (new construction; excluding small, rubber & plastic boats)	1,341	8,039	18,431	29,150	14,099	**71,060**
Machine Guns	126,113	666,820	830,384	798,782	302,798	**2,724,897**
Tanks	4,258	23,884	29,497	17,565	11,184	**86,388**

The Call is Answered

(Source: *The Homefront*, by Archie Satterfield, New York: The Playboy Press, 1981, page 193)

Jobs were easy to get. They'd hire anyone and wouldn't fire anyone. One summer I decided to work at an aircraft company, and they hired me at sixteen. I wanted to learn how to buck rivets, and, boy, did I learn. You'd stand on the other side from the riveter and hold a bar against the back of the metal and the impact of the rivet gun against the bar flattened the rivet. We got 82 1/2 cents an hour and we were rich.

We put air bolts on the B-17s as they came down the assembly line. Then they transferred me over to the B-29s on a super-secret section with engineers running around all over the place because it

15

was only the third or fourth B-29 they'd built. One of the main reasons they brought me in was because I was so small I could get into the tight places to buck these rivets...

— Unidentified Teenager

❖ ❖ ❖ ❖ ❖ ❖

(Source: Harris, Mitchell, Schechter, *op. cit.,* pages 161-162)

...Many a time the men would work eight hours and you needed some of them, the experienced ones, to get the ship out in time. So we'd ask who would care to work straight on through. And just about everybody there would volunteer and work until they could almost go to sleep on the job. Many times I had to work sixteen hours without stopping, down in a cold drydock, to make sure everything got done. When your eight-hour shift was up, you just didn't stop if you knew that ship had to catch a convoy.

We not only worked twelve, sixteen hours a day, but lots of weeks and months we wouldn't even have a day off. We never minded working seven days or what our hours were, for while we were working in the yard the people aboard the ships were out there actually fighting. It made us feel like we were only sacrificing a little bit. Your best friend might be out there on one of those ships, maybe getting bombed. You felt like you had to help him while he was out there helping you.

...When the war broke out, and I saw what people could do when they all pulled together, and the sacrifices they were willing to make, it made me really love this country again. It made you think you were living in a great country. It made you proud to be an American...

— William Pefley

Daily Life
by
Phyllis Raybin Emert

The average family in 1941 prewar America earned from $2,000 to just under $3,000 a year. Minimum wage was 40 cents an hour, but agricultural and domestic workers earned 15 cents or less an hour. Four million people were still out of work nationally.

A new car was a major investment for most families. A 1941 Chevrolet sold for $700 while a luxurious Oldsmobile cost $1,100. Women's silk stockings were 89 cents a pair and a new vacuum cleaner sold for $15.95.

Each night Americans gathered around their radio sets to listen to the antics of Jack Benny or ventriloquist Edgar Bergen and his dummy pal, Charlie McCarthy. People sang popular tunes like "The Last Time I Saw Paris," and "Chattanooga Choo Choo" or went to the movies for 25 cents to laugh at a double bill of Abbot and Costello in "Buck Private" and "Keep 'Em Flying."

Life changed dramatically after this country's entrance into the war in 1941. Scarcity and shortages became regular topics of conversation, but people also talked of sacrifice, patriotism, and victory.

A carefully orchestrated barrage of positive propaganda by government, business, and the entertainment industry combined to personalize the war for Americans. "Doing without" was a way of supporting the troops, and many of the men, women, and children at home believed strongly that they were contributing to the war effort by doing their fair share.

The Office of Price Administration (OPA) was created by President Roosevelt to develop a plan for rationing consumer goods needed for the war and establishing price controls to combat inflation (the rise of prices). The OPA used a system of certificate rationing for scarce single items, coupon rationing for other items such as shoes, sugar, and coffee, and point rationing for meats, butter, cheese, and canned goods.

Americans turned in their old tires and other rubber products needed for war-time production. New tires and retreads were strictly rationed.

With the world's rubber supplies cut off by Japanese conquests in the Far East, the government issued a freeze on tires and a ban on re-capping old ones. The President urged all Americans to turn in all their rubber, to lower their automobile speed and to drive only to and from work in an effort to conserve their tires. Certificate ration-ing of tires was put into effect immediately and heating oil and gaso-line rationing followed soon after.

The OPA established thousands of rationing boards across the country and every family received ration books with various colored stamps and coupons. An "A" sticker allowed a family four (later three) gallons of gas each week. A "B" sticker was for those who had extra driving such as war plant workers or car pool drivers. A "C" sticker was usually for those who performed what was termed essential activities, while "E" or "X" stickers or cards, which allowed unlimited gas, were reserved for policemen, firemen and politicians. The result of gasoline rationing was that Americans traveled less and traffic fatalities decreased. When people traveled, they used public forms of transportation such as trains and buses.

Each person was allowed 28 ounces of meat and 4 ounces of cheese per week, much lower than prewar years. Now most of America's meats and cheeses went to feed the more than 15 million servicemen fighting in Europe and in the Pacific.

Although frustrated at first, Americans quickly adapted to the new rationing system, convinced that food was "a weapon of war." Most believed that rationing allowed all families to have their fair share and that it helped to prevent the hoarding of food and supplies by certain individuals.

The shortages and rationing impacted every family and challenged each housewife to come up with new and innovative ways to cook without the basics of sugar, butter, and meat. Main dishes of beans, vegetables and eggs became commonplace. Margarine became a popular butter substitute. Alternative sweeteners such as honey were used whenever possible. In some places, horsemeat replaced beef, while some restaurants offered buffalo and antelope instead.

Housewives were encouraged to save used cooking fat and turn it in to the local meat dealer. These kitchen fats were made into glycerine which make up the main ingredient in powder charges for shells and other munitions.

Coffee drinkers were limited to less than a cup a day and cigarettes, most of which went to the military, were hard to come by.

Shopping became a skill and grocery stores were often crowded with people looking for scarce items with just the right amount of coupons or points.

A black market for goods and supplies existed during the war years. If people were willing to pay enough, scarce items in short supply could be procured by wealthier Americans. The average family dabbled in the black market only occasionally when their neighborhood grocer might save them a special cut of meat or a can of vegetables for important occasions.

Now women made do with bare legs instead of stockings, since silk was diverted to the making of parachutes. To conserve fabric, women's skirts were shortened to an inch above the knee and they often wore short sleeves. Shorter men's jackets were now designed with narrower lapels, no vests, and pants were worn without cuffs.

The government encouraged scrap paper, tin foil, and scrap metal drives. At the urging of President Roosevelt, more than 20 million Americans planted victory gardens and ate and canned their own vegetables. To pay for the enormous cost of the war, there were numerous War Bond drives and the government imposed a 5 per cent surcharge on all income taxes (called a Victory tax).

The Office of Civilian Defense (OCD) was created by America's entrance into the war. Its main job was to protect the civilian population in the event of an enemy attack. The OCD recruited millions of volunteers to serve as air-raid wardens, who were in charge of keeping all lights off during blackouts. Other civilian volunteer groups included the Ground Observer Corps (GOC) whose main role was to watch for enemy aircraft along the coastlines and the Civil Air Patrol (CAP) which consisted of overage or retired pilots who flew submarine-patrol duty in the Atlantic.

Although early fears of an enemy attack on the continental United States were, for the most part, groundless, several incidents did occur during the war years which were purposely not well-publicized by the government for obvious reasons.

In the fall of 1942, Flying Officer Nobuo Fujita of the Imperial Japanese Navy flew a Mitsubishi Zero fighter plane over a forested area of Oregon and dropped several incendiary bombs. The Zero had been carried across the Pacific in a watertight compartment of an enemy submarine and fitted with pontoon floats so it could take off on the surface of the ocean. The purpose of the mission was to set off a disruptive firestorm but the bombs did little damage. After two attacks, both of which were unsuccessful, Fujita gave up and returned to the submarine. He was the only enemy pilot to bomb the United States during World War II.

Eight German saboteurs were arrested and imprisoned after German U-boats brought four of them off the coast of Long Island, New York and another four off the Florida coast in mid-1942. The men came ashore in rubber rafts and intended to blow up American aluminum plants and railroads throughout the country.

Japanese bombs did cause six civilian deaths on American soil in early 1945. Japan launched thousands of large paper balloons, each carrying several 30-pound bombs which were set to go off three to five days later. The balloons crossed the Pacific by riding the fast-moving high-altitude air currents. About 300 actually reached the West Coast and most failed to explode. One of these balloon bombs landed on Mount Gearhart in Oregon, killing a woman and five local children who were out camping that day in the area. These six deaths were the only known casualties on the home front caused by enemy weapons during World War II.

War news became a top priority in the daily life of all Americans. Major radio stations increased news shows to more than 20 per cent of their total programming. The war touched every aspect of life. Comic book heroes and newspaper comic strip characters even went to war. Among others, Joe Palooka enlisted in the Army as a private first class and Dick Tracy became an officer for Naval Intelligence.

Popular music, Hollywood movies and Broadway shows had patriotic military themes. Americans sang such songs as "Praise the Lord and Pass the Ammunition," and "Goodbye Mama, I'm Off to Yokohama." They saw films like "Casablanca," "The Sands of Iwo Jima," and "Wake Island." On Broadway, Irving Berlin's "This is The Army" advertised a cast of 300 soldiers in a musical salute to the Army.

Despite the scarcity and the shortages, the rationing and the sacrifices, there was a special feeling of patriotism and unity in most Americans that had never before existed to such an extent. Ronald H. Bailey, editor of *The Home Front: USA* said it best. "Life as never before, had a direction and a purpose."

The following excerpts focus on all aspects of daily life in America during the war years — from Presidential proclamations to advertisements to reminiscences of those who lived through it.

———————————————

(Source: Rosenman, *1942 - Humanity on the Defensive, op. cit.,* pages 230, 271-273)

...There is one front and one battle where everyone in the United States — every man, woman, and child — is in action, and will be privileged to remain in action throughout this war. That front is right here at home, in our daily lives, and in our daily tasks. Here at home everyone will have the privilege of making whatever self-denial is necessary, not only to supply our fighting men, but to keep the economic structure of our country fortified and secure during the war and after the war...

— President Franklin D. Roosevelt
Fireside Chat - April, 1942

Cartoon drawing by O. Soglow. (OWI). National Archives.

❖ ❖ ❖ ❖ ❖ ❖

...Rubber is a problem for this reason — because modern wars cannot be won without rubber and because 92 percent of our normal supply of rubber has been cut off by the Japanese...

It is not the Army and Navy alone which need rubber. The process of production also needs rubber. We need rubber to get our war workers back and forth to their plants — some of them far from workers' homes. We need rubber to keep our essential goods and supplies moving...

...We have asked the filling station operators — the thousands upon thousands of citizens who operate gas stations and garages from one end of the country to the other — to help. And they have generously and patriotically agreed to help: they and the oil companies which serve them.

They have agreed to take the old rubber in and to pay for it at the standard rate of a penny a pound — an amount which will later be refunded to them by the Government.

I know that I don't need to urge you to take part in this collection drive. All you need to know is the place to take your rubber and the time to take it there — and the fact that your country needs it...

We do want every bit of rubber you can possibly spare — and in any quantity — less than a pound — many pounds. We want it in every form — old tires, old rubber raincoats, old garden hose, rubber shoes, bathing caps, gloves — whatever you have that is made of rubber...

One thing you can be sure of — we are going to see to it that there is enough rubber to build the planes to bomb Tokyo and Berlin — enough rubber to build the tanks to crush the enemy wherever we may find him — enough rubber to win this war...

> — President Franklin D. Roosevelt
> Radio Address on Scrap Rubber
> June 12, 1942

❖ ❖ ❖ ❖ ❖ ❖

(Source: Satterfield, *op. cit.*, pages 200-201)

Each person, regardless of age, will be allowed sixteen points a week for the whole group of new items to be rationed. There will be no exact meat ration, although...the amount of meat available will average two pounds per week per person for home consumption.

Restaurants will continue to be coupon-free to the customers, although OPA will ration the supplies used by restaurants.

Bouillon cubes and beef extracts, not rationed now with canned soup, will be rationed with meat.

Not all cheeses will be rationed. Hard cheese like Swiss and American will be rationed; soft or perishable cheese like cream cheese, cottage cheese, Camembert and Brie will not be rationed.

Canned fish will be rationed, but fresh, frozen, smoked, salt and pickled fish will not be rationed.

Weekly coupons will be good for a month. If any coupons are left over from the first week, they may be used with the second week's coupons...

Blue Stamps in War Ration Book No. 2 are used for most canned goods and for dried peas, beans, lentils, and frozen commodities like fruit juice. The Red Stamps are used for meats, canned fish, butter, cheese, edible fats, and canned milk. You have to give up more points when buying scarce foods than when buying the same quantity of a more plentiful one...

> — *Associated Press*
> Office of Price Administration directives
> March 12, 1943

❖ ❖ ❖ ❖ ❖ ❖

...I hope every American who possibly can will grow a victory garden this year. We found out last year that even the small gardens helped.

The total harvest from victory gardens was tremendous. It made the difference between scarcity and abundance. The Department of Agriculture surveys show that 42 percent of the fresh vegetables consumed in 1943 came from victory gardens. This should clearly emphasize the far-reaching importance of the victory garden program.

Because of the greatly increased demands in 1944, we will need all the food we can grow. Food still remains a first essential to winning the war. Victory gardens are of direct benefit in helping relieve manpower, transportation, and living costs as well as the food problem. Increased food requirements for our armed forces and our allies give every citizen an opportunity to do something toward backing up the boys at the front.

> — President Franklin D. Roosevelt
> Message to the American People
> April 1, 1944

❖ ❖ ❖ ❖ ❖ ❖

(Source: *Produce and Conserve, Share and Play Square*, edited by Barbara McLean Ward, Portsmouth, New Hampshire: Strawberry Banke Museum and University Press of New England, 1994, page 175)

Printed Poster

Office of Economic Stabilization, Washington D.C.

I'M OUT TO LICK RUNAWAY PRICES
Let's All Follow the 7-Key Plan to Hold Prices Down

1. Buy and hold War Bonds
2. Pay willingly our share of taxes.
3. Provide adequate life insurance and savings for our future
4. Reduce our debts as much as possible
5. Buy only what we need and make what we have last longer
6. Follow ration rules and price ceilings
7. Cooperate with our Government's wage stabilization program

(1943)

"We'll Knock the Japs Right into the
Laps of the Nazis"

(Song introduced by Burt Wheeler on December 7, 1941)

(Source: *Don't You Know There's a War On?* by Richard R. Lingeman, New York: G.P. Putnam's Sons, 1970, page 211)

Oh, we didn't want to do it but they're asking for it now
So, we'll knock the Japs right into the laps of the Nazis,
When they hop on Honolulu, that's a thing we won't allow
So we'll knock the Japs right into the laps of the Nazis!
Chins up, Yankees, let's see it through
And show them there's no yellow in the red, white and blue.
I'd hate to be in Yokohama when our brothers make their bow,
For we'll knock the Japs right into the laps of the Nazis!

❖ ❖ ❖ ❖ ❖ ❖

(Source: Satterfield, *op. cit.,* pages 179, 187)

Gasoline was the biggest problem for a teenager. We still had cars, and gasoline was our biggest worry of all the rationing. We'd always pick up our dates in sequence when we had gas, and you might end up not taking your date home if it would save gas for you to be dropped off first. You'd kiss your date goodnight in front of your house, not hers...

— Unidentified

❖ ❖ ❖ ❖ ❖ ❖

Death got to be a common thing with us. Every day they'd have a big list in the paper and a friend might be on the list. At the time you'd think it was too bad, but you got so saturated with deaths and people missing that you just accepted it as natural. It went on and on and on for four years...

— Unidentified

❖ ❖ ❖ ❖ ❖ ❖

(Source: Harris, Mitchell, Schechter, *op cit.*, pages 69-70)

...We lived only three blocks from the beach, and before the war started we would walk down there with our mother and play in the waves and sand. But during the war the whole coast was blocked off from civilian use. All along the bluffs, they set up giant antiaircraft artillery and camouflage netting which to a small child appeared to be several stories high. You couldn't see the ocean anymore. All you could see was the guns and camouflage.

We also had air raid alerts which made the possibility of invasion seem very real. Because Pearl Harbor had been bombed and California was on the Pacific and close to the Japanese, we felt we could have a surprise air attack at any minute...

Besides the fear, the war also created a sense of distrust. I can remember posters everywhere with Uncle Sam holding a finger up to his lips, "SHHH." Don't give away secrets. "Loose lips sink ships." You weren't supposed to trust anyone. You heard it on the radio, saw it in the movies. They'd tell you even the nicest person could turn out to be a spy.

Yet, at the same time, there were also a lot of positive things about the war, a kind of game atmosphere and team spirit. I remember all the neighborhood women sitting around the kitchen table pooling and trading ration coupons. My grandmother raised chickens so we often didn't need our meat coupons. And we made our own butter. So one month we might trade our meat or dairy coupons for sugar. The next month we might trade our sugar for steak or nylons. I know rationing was sometimes a hardship to my mother, but as a child seeing all these coupons trading back and forth, it was like watching a big Monopoly game...

— Sheril Jankovsky Cunning

Women in Wartime

by
Phyllis Raybin Emert

In 1941, most Americans firmly believed that a woman's place was in the home caring for her husband and children as a wife and mother. Although more than 15% of all married women (about 12 million) worked outside of the home, it was because of economic necessity and not by choice.

In the months after Pearl Harbor, with millions of men in uniform and increased weapons production a top priority and critical necessity, American industry turned to women to meet the shortage of war workers on the home front.

President Franklin D. Roosevelt stated in 1942, "in some communities employers dislike to hire women. In others they are reluctant to hire Negroes. We can no longer afford to indulge such prejudice."

Between 1940 and 1944, more than 6 million additional women (single, married, black, white, Hispanic, young and old) joined the work force. Many of them worked in non-traditional factory jobs in the aircraft and shipbuilding industries.

Women became welders, operated blast furnaces and drill presses and ran forklifts. "Rosie the Riveter" was a popular wartime symbol of a strong woman who helped in the war effort but still maintained her femininity.

Although women performed the same work as men in the factories, they were not paid the same salaries. Men received higher wages for the same work. Most managerial and supervisory jobs were still held by men. The women were thought of as temporary substitute workers until the men returned.

This World War II poster, commissioned by the War Production Coordinating Committee, features Rosie the Riveter. National Archives.

At the same time, more than a quarter of a million women joined the various branches of the military. For the first time ever, they served in non-combat positions other than that of nurse.

No matter how skillful or successful women were at their jobs, they encountered sexism (discrimination) both at work and at home. Insecure male war workers were frequently hostile to their female colleagues. Many feared women were turning into masculine Amazons and threatened their status as men.

Working women with families were expected to perform all the domestic tasks of a non-working woman, including grocery shopping, cooking, cleaning and caring for the children, in addition to putting in an 8 to 10 hour shift at the plant.

When juvenile delinquency and truancy rates increased dramatically during the war years, working women were blamed for a lack of parental supervision. Child care became an important issue. Some factories, such as Douglas Aircraft and Kaiser shipyards, and certain cities that obtained federal assistance, set up day care centers and nursery schools to care for the young children of working mothers. Most women, however, depended on other family members to watch their children while they were at work.

As a group, black women benefited the most from increased wartime employment. Nearly half worked outside the home before the war, almost 60% of them in private domestic service as housecleaners, maids, and cooks with no benefits. After the war that number dropped significantly to 40%. When jobs opened up in the factories, black women were more than eager to accept these higher paying positions with benefits. They also were hired in large numbers by the federal government in clerical and administrative positions.

As the war wound down, massive layoffs of women occurred in the war industries. Although many returned to their original role of full time homemaker and mother, others found employment in white collar office jobs such as bookkeeper and bank teller, which had traditionally been held by men prior to the war.

(Source: *Rosie the Riveter Revisited*, by Sherna Berger Gluck, Boston: Twayne Publishers, 1987, pages 62, 63, 65)

...It was July when I went to work. I started at 52.5 cents an hour. I thought I'd hit the mother lode!

That was the first time I'd ever worn slacks...If you worked with any of the machinery, you were supposed to wear a hair net, and if you were working around welding, you wore goggles...

The planes that Vultee put out, they weren't these big bombers; they were... two-seater planes...

...I went into subassembly. They had these "skins": sheets of aluminum about four feet by eight feet. These were riveted on to the sides of the plane. But they had to be cleaned. They had two tanks, one a rinse tank with clear water and one with a real strong acid. We wore big heavy rubber gloves that came way up our arms. We dipped these skins in this acid and we had to take a cloth and swab it around. Then we'd rinse them in the clear tank and stand them up on the floor and dry them with an air hose. Then they were taken over to the spot-weld machines.

After a few days I was kind of in charge of the tanks...

After a while, the supervisor wanted me to go on the spot-welding machine...but the men got all up in arms. They didn't want any women on there and they all protested. So I didn't get on the spot-welding machine... Later, I heard that there was a vacancy over in the machine shop...

...They started me out on a Harding lathe, which was a little, small lathe. I guess maybe the whole thing was about five foot. They didn't do too many operations on those; it was more like cutting rods to a certain length, which was very simple. I worked for a few months on that and on the drill press, and then I got a chance to go on one of the big lathes, the number three — the number fives were the big ones. I really liked that.

...Right in my own department, they never did put women on the really big, number five lathes...Class A machinists were still men. The women got to be Class B machinists, which was as much as we expected to be. We weren't making a career of it like men. We were doing what was there to do...

It just ended overnight. My daughter had been visiting her aunt for the summer down in New Mexico, and I had taken a week's vacation and gone down to bring her back. The war ended while I was down there. By the time I got back, I had a telegram saying that the job was over...

— Marye Stumph

Young woman working at the Kaiser shipyard. National Archives (OWI)

❖ ❖ ❖ ❖ ❖ ❖

(Source: Gluck, *ibid.,* page 100)

American women are learning how to put planes and tanks together, how to read blueprints, how to weld and rivet and make the great machinery of war production hum under skillful eyes and hands. But they're also learning how to look smart in overalls and how to be glamorous after work. They are learning to fulfill both the useful and the beautiful ideal.

— Woman's Home Companion, October 19, 1943

❖ ❖ ❖ ❖ ❖ ❖

"Her Seven Jobs All Help Win the War"

(Source: Ward, *op cit.*, page 36)

1. **WIFE!** She knows that her husband can carry on the war pace of his job only if she keeps his home a peaceful, happy place. She's a loving and lovable person, doing a fine job of home-making. A salute for being that kind of wife.

2. **MOTHER!** She guards her youngsters' health, body, and mind. She sees they get foods from the "Basic 7" Nutritional Groups daily. Sensing their shock from wartime headlines, she calmly explains why American men go off to fight.

3. **PURCHASING AGENT!** She realizes rationing means fair sharing. She sympathizes with dealers — understands why she often cannot get just the cut she wants, or the Swift's brands of beef or other meats she'd prefer to have.

4. **COOK!** She cooks with care to save nutritive values. She makes the most of meat; reduces shrinkage by cooking at low temperature; prepares attractive dishes from leftovers; learns to cook every kind of cut so it will taste its very best.

5. **SALVAGE EXPERT!** She wastes nothing, for she knows that Food Fights for Freedom. She uses every bit of leftovers, even bones are saved for soup. She regularly takes to her dealer the drippings of fat that have no further cooking use.

6. **WAR WORKER!** She joins wholeheartedly in the community projects of civilian defense. She sends neat bandages on far errands of mercy. And (to her it is a matter of special pride) the honored list of blood donors includes her name.

7. **WAR BOND BUYER!** She does without things she wants so our men will have the things they need. Over 10% of her husband's pay goes for War Bonds, plus dollars she saves in her household budget. Swift salutes Mrs. America, Patriot.

— Swift's Brands of Beef Advertisement
Good Housekeeping, January, 1944

❖ ❖ ❖ ❖ ❖ ❖

(Source: Hoehling, *op. cit.*, pages 59-61)

It was the early part of December of 1942 that I made up my mind I would like to work in the shipyards. The reason I chose welding was because my husband was a welder and liked it very much. I went to the employment office. There were just lines of people waiting to get signed up in all crafts. They sent me to school for two weeks...

I'll never forget the first night at school: all them leathers! I felt like I was a deep-sea diver: jacket and overalls, hood which certainly covered your face and head. A hairdo meant nothing. You had to have your hair completely covered if you wanted any left, long gloves (up to your elbows), still those little sparks had a way of finding you.

We learned to weld overhead which was quite hard holding your arms... and enough welding lead higher than your head. Of course the longer you welded the more you could weld. I'll admit it was good exercise. Vertical wasn't so hard. A lot of time we could sit down for this. Flat — we felt we were sailing when we had to weld flat.

...My first job was on the outfitting dock. They were pretty well finished. Just pick-up jobs and so...

The first ones I worked on we stood on the upper deck and looked down. They were huge! They carried jeeps and tanks. The kitchens were all of stainless, small but beautiful. Just as you would get attached to them they went out to sea. Then we would start all over finishing another one which had been launched.

We changed again and made escort vessels. They sent most of the women to the plate shop. That was the beginning of the ships. You could see no progress as we'd weld two pieces together. This piece was taken to the ways to be put together forming another ship. I didn't care for the shop at all. It was off to itself. As soon as I could I asked for a transfer. I was then put on the ways. It was here you could see the ship forming. We did all but the finishing touches — Christened with a bottle of champagne, sent down the ways into the water. It gave you quite a thrill to think you were helping win the war...such a small part but I was helping.

I worked as a welder for 32 months, was one of the last women to be laid off, which was the latter part of July, 1945. It was nice to be home again...   — Edith Long

❖ ❖ ❖ ❖ ❖ ❖

(Source: Harris, Mitchell, Schechter, *op. cit.*, pages 134-136)

...I really wanted to help the war effort. I could have worked for the Red Cross and rolled bandages, but I wanted to do something that I thought was really vital. Building bombers was, so I answered an ad for Boeing.

My mother was horrified... My father was horrified, too, no matter how I tried to impress on him that this was a war effort on my part... My husband thought it was utterly ridiculous. I had never worked. I didn't know how to handle money, as he put it...but he was wrong.

They started me as a clerk in this huge toolroom. I had never handled a tool in my life outside of a hammer...

I started at Boeing at forty-six and a half cents an hour. That was remarkable, women working and earning that sort of pay. After I had worked there a few months, Boeing themselves upped my salary to sixty-two and a half cents an hour, which was really thrilling. No one would believe it, myself least of all. From then on I had steady increases. Eventually I became chief clerk of the toolroom. I think I was the first woman chief clerk they had.

...I learned that just because you're a woman and have never worked is no reason you can't learn. The job really broadened me. I had led a very sheltered life. I had had no contact with Negroes except as maids or gardeners... I found that some of the black people I got to know there were very superior, and certainly equal to me — equal to anyone I ever knew. I learned that color has nothing at all to do with ability...

                                                    — Inez Sauer

Women As Proportion Of All Workers, By Occupational Status, 1940-1947

(Source: Women's Bureau, *Women as Workers, A Statistical Guide.* Washington, D.C. 1953, pages 15-17, from *Women at War with America* by D'Ann Campbell. Cambridge, Massachusetts: Harvard University Press, 1984, page 239)

Occupation	1940 (%)	1945 (%)	1947(%)
Professional	45.5	46.5	39.9
Managerial	11.7	17.4	13.5
Clerical	52.6	70.3	58.6
Sales	27.9	54.1	39.9
All white collar	35.8	49.6	38.9
Craftsman, foreman, skilled	2.1	4.4	2.1
Factory operative	25.7	38.3	28.1
Domestic service	93.8	93.8	92.3
Other service	40.1	47.8	43.6
All blue collar	26.2	31.7	24.6
Agriculture	8.0	22.4	11.8
All occupations	25.9	36.0	27.9

❖ ❖ ❖ ❖ ❖ ❖

(Source: Gluck, *op. cit.*, pages 38-39, 42-43, 49)

...They [North American Aviation] had fifteen or twenty departments, but all the Negroes went to Department 17 because there was nothing but shooting and bucking rivets. You stood on one side of the panel and your partner stood on this side, and he would shoot the rivets with a gun and you'd buck them with the bar... I stayed in it about two or three weeks and then I just decided I did *not* like that. I went and told my foreman and he didn't do anything about it, so I decided I'd leave.

While I was standing out on the railroad track, I ran into somebody else out there fussing also. I went over to the union and they told me what to do. I went back inside and they sent me to another department where you did bench work and I liked that much better...

I must have stayed there nearly a year, and then they put me over in another department, "Plastics." It was the tail section of the B-Bomber, the Billy Mitchell Bomber. I put a little part in the gunsight. You had a little ratchet set and you would screw it in there. Then I cleaned the top of the glass off and put a piece of paper over it to seal it off to go to the next section. I worked over there until the end of the war. Well, not quite the end, because I got pregnant, and while I was off having the baby the war was over.

...I worked the day shift and my sister worked the night shift. I worked ten hours a day for five days a week...

...My sister always said... "Hitler was the one that got us out of the white folks' kitchen"....

There were some departments, they didn't even allow a black person to walk through there let alone work in there. Some of the white people did not want to work with the Negro. They had arguments right there. Sometimes they would get fired and walk on out the door, but it was one more white person gone...

38

We always talking about women's lib and working. Well, we all know that the Negro woman was the first woman that left home to go to work. She's been working ever since because she had to work beside her husband in slavery — against her will. So she has always worked... She has really pioneered the field. Then after we've gotten out here and proved that it can be done, then the white woman decided, "Hey, I don't want to stay home and do nothing." She zeroed in on the best jobs. So we're still on the tail-end, but we still back there fighting.

— Fanny Christina Hill

❖ ❖ ❖ ❖ ❖ ❖

(Source: Gluck, *ibid.,* page 230)

...There were eighteen girls working...and eight of them were Negro girls. There were men, too, because the rudders and all that went on right there in the department. After we finished the boots on the stabilizers, then the men put them on the tail sections of the plane. But I just supervised the women.

There was a leadman, a foreman, and an assistant foreman over me, but I had to see if the girls were working and get supplies to do the work and see if they got along. There was a girl from the South. I guess she had never been around Negroes and she didn't want to work near them. I told her I had four brothers out in the Pacific and they were all fighting at the same time, and why couldn't she stand in there and work next to someone no matter who they were? Kind of made me a little angry...

— Marie Baker

❖ ❖ ❖ ❖ ❖ ❖

(Source: Gluck, *ibid.,* pages 135-136)

...I went to work for Kreager Oil Company... They gave me a uniform everyday and soap to wash the grease off my hands, and they taught me how to do batteries. It was very simple, very easy: check the oil, wipe the windshield, put the gas in, get the money, get the coupon.

I worked for six months and everyday someone came in saying, "Do you want a job?" My head was going crazy. They were recruiting for any kind of work you wanted. Newspapers, just splashed everywhere: "Help Wanted," "Help Wanted," "Jobs," "Jobs," "Jobs." Propaganda on every radio station: "If you're an American citizen, come to gate so-and-so" — at Lockheed or at the shipyards in San Pedro. And they did it on the movie screens when they'd pass the collection cans. You were bombarded.

They were begging for workers. They didn't care whether you were black, white, young, old... I had so much work offered to me and I was not even qualified — I just had the capability of learning very fast. Within three weeks of coming to California my mind was dazzled with all the offers I had...

Actually what attracted me — it was not the money and it was not the job because I didn't even know how much money I was going to make. But the ads... "Do Your Part," "Uncle Sam Needs You," "V for Victory." I got caught up in that patriotic "win the war," "help the boys..."

Anyhow, Vega Aircraft was the first one I learned about... I called this girl I had met and we went together. We both went for the same job, but she was immediately hired for a more educated job because she had finished high school. I went on the assembly line...

— Juanita Loveless

Injustice And Racism

by
Phyllis Raybin Emert

Japanese Americans

After the unprovoked attack on Pearl Harbor, distrust, fear, and anger against the approximately 130,000 Japanese Americans living in the United States erupted and intensified, especially in California where an enemy invasion was believed imminent. Nearly 115,000 Japanese lived in the Golden State. The presence of so many Issei (those born in Japan who immigrated to America) and Nisei (second-generation natural-born U.S. citizens of Japanese descent) was believed to constitute a security threat.

Many Californians questioned the loyalty and allegiance of these Japanese and worried whether they would resort to sabotage or treason to aid the enemies of America. Prominent citizens such as General John L. DeWitt, Governor Culbert Olson and State Attorney General Earl Warren supported the idea of a mass evacuation of all Japanese from the West Coast. They were indifferent to the fact that about 80,000 Nisei were American citizens and such a forced removal meant depriving them of their civil liberties and due process under the law.

In an attempt to understand why level-headed American leaders would promote racism over civil rights, one needs to take into account the fear and hysteria that was prevalent in the months following Pearl Harbor. However, distrust and antagonism against the Japanese was not a new phenomenon, but firmly rooted in California's history.

The state's Anti-Alien Land Law of 1923 and the federal Oriental

Exclusion Act of 1924 combined to cut off the flow of immigrants from Asia and prohibited Japanese from becoming naturalized citizens or owning land. Although Issei couldn't own property themselves, they could purchase property in their children's names.

The post-Pearl Harbor hysteria coupled with the historical suspicion and hatred against the Japanese convinced President Roosevelt to sign Executive Order 9066 which authorized the establishment of military areas on the West Coast from which "any or all persons could be removed."

An often asked question is why the hatred focused on Japanese Americans and not German or Italian Americans? Many believe the answer is racism. The Japanese were not Caucasians. They looked different and didn't assimilate into American society as easily as other white ethnic groups. The Japanese preferred to live together in their own areas and practice their own traditions while German and Italian Americans tended to blend more into American society. It was hard to tell a German from a Nebraskan and baseball star Joe Di Maggio and well-known singer Frank Sinatra, both of Italian descent, were popular American celebrities.

According to Ronald H. Bailey in *The Home Front: U.S.A.*, about 5,000 German and Italian Americans were rounded up and interned by the government, but most were released within a year. Americans tended to blame Hitler and Mussolini for the war and not necessarily the German and Italian people. But the surprise attack at Pearl Harbor made it more personal. This, coupled with the fact that the Japanese were of a different race, as Bailey noted, "tended to blur the distinction between the people and their leaders."

After Executive Order 9066, the Tolan Committee (formed by Congress) found that a voluntary resettlement of all Japanese from coastal areas to inland states was not feasible. Most of the governors would not allow them into their states except under armed guard. The Tolan Committee recommended a federal agency to oversee the Japanese removal and to establish internment camps. The War Relocation Authority (WRA) was formed in March of 1942 and was responsible for building and supervising the camps.

Beginning on March 22, 1942, about 110,000 Japanese were transported to 15 temporary assembly centers in California, Oregon, Washington and Arizona. A few months later, they were moved to ten permanent relocation centers scattered throughout the country. The Tule Lake camp near Newell, California was used especially for those evacuees who claimed loyalty to Japan and not the United States. But, the vast majority were loyal Americans and to prove it, they cooperated fully with their government.

Given little or no opportunity to dispose of their homes, businesses or belongings, the Japanese lost nearly everything they owned. They sold out to their white neighbors at rock bottom prices and were only allowed to take what they could carry to the assembly centers. Many successful Japanese American farmers (a source of envy by white vegetable farmers) were forced to abandon their land and their crops.

Once at the permanent relocation centers, food and shelter were provided, but living conditions were overcrowded and generally poor. Barbed wire fences surrounded the camps and guards with rifles were always in evidence. Wages from $12 to $21 per month were paid to those who wished to work. Residents of the camps built their own furniture, ran the schools, organized clubs, staffed their own newspaper and formed Community Councils.

As time passed some Nisei were allowed to leave the camps for seasonal agricultural employment or to attend colleges in the east. Others enlisted in the armed forces and fought in the all-Nisei 442nd Regimental Combat Group - the most decorated (and highest casualty rate) in military service.

Most of the Japanese remained in the camps throughout the war years. The last of the centers was closed in March, 1946. It's been estimated that internees suffered losses of over $400 million. Although the entire evacuation and internment episode was considered a mistake after the war, it wasn't until 1982 that a federal commission formally announced that it was "a grave injustice."

In 1988, President Ronald Reagan signed a bill which publicly apologized to the Japanese American internees during the war and gave each of the 60,000 survivors a tax-free payment of $20,000.

It is significant to note that not a single Japanese American was ever indicted or brought to trial on charges of treason, espionage or sabotage during World War II!

African Americans

Another group directly affected by injustice and racism during the war years was America's 13 million African Americans. In their continuing struggle for equality, they were faced with discrimination and prejudice in the armed forces, the labor unions and in defense industries.

Many draft boards refused to accept blacks, believing they were not capable of fighting on an equal level with whites. The Army accepted a limited number and kept them in segregated units as laborers. The Army Air Force as well as the Marines and the Coast Guard were limited to whites only. The Navy accepted even fewer black men than the Army and most served as messmen or cooks.

The wartime migration of Southern white workers to factory towns and big cities aggravated the racial situation since they brought with them the civil war mentality that blacks were naturally inferior to others. In addition, many military training camps were located in the South and African Americans faced discrimination, prejudice, and even outbreaks of racial violence, on a regular basis. All activities were segregated. Some posts held special all-black dances or other events, and military chapels even had special services for African Americans.

The American Red Cross went so far as to separate blood plasma into "white" and "colored" bottles, not realizing that a scientist named Dr. Charles Drew, himself an African American, perfected the process of preserving plasma.

Even more disgraceful and humiliating was the story of a restaurant in Salina, Kansas which served food to German prisoners of war, yet refused to serve black men in uniform!

Many trade unions were all-white or segregated their black members. Most defense industry jobs for blacks were at the lowest levels and white workers threatened to strike if blacks were promoted or upgraded.

During World War II, black leaders and organizations like the National Association for the Advancement of Colored People (NAACP) with the support of the black press, organized a "Double V" campaign calling for victory against the fascist enemy overseas and victory against racism at home. African Americans responded in what turned out to be the beginning of the modern civil rights movement.

A threatened march on Washington in 1941 protesting the lack of job opportunities for blacks in defense industries was cancelled after President Franklin D. Roosevelt issued Executive Order 8802. This was the first governmental order on behalf of equal rights since the Emancipation Proclamation during the Civil War. It prohibited discrimination in employment practices by the federal government and by all labor unions and industries involved in war-related work. Executive Order 8802 also established the Fair Employment Practices Commission (FEPC) to enforce this policy.

The FEPC intervened in Philadelphia in 1944 when white trolley-car drivers, angered when the company hired eight black drivers, went on a city-wide strike, shutting down the public transportation system. President Roosevelt called in federal troops to break the strike and keep the trolleys running. The white drivers soon returned to their jobs and the black drivers were peacefully accepted.

In general, African Americans as a group benefited during the war years. The number of blacks in industry jobs nearly tripled from half a million in 1940 to nearly 1 1/2 million in 1945. Large numbers found work in the federal government and membership in labor unions doubled to more than a million members.

The average salary increase for African-Americans during the war nearly quadrupled. According to Barbara McLean Ward, who edited the book *Produce and Conserve, Share and Play Square*, wages increased from $457 to $1976 a year, still noticeably lower than the gains made by white workers whose average salary went from $1064 to $2600 a year.

Discontent rose among whites as blacks became more militant in their stand against racial discrimination and their lower economic and social position in American society. Blacks became increasingly angered at the hypocrisy of fighting Nazi racism in Europe while discrimination raged on the home front.

As blacks made small advances, white opposition increased and violence erupted between the races in dozens of cities in 1943, including New York, Detroit and Los Angeles. In Detroit alone, nine whites and 25 blacks were killed before federal troops brought peace to the city!

President Roosevelt's Executive Order 9279 in December, 1942 required that all the military services end restrictions on accepting blacks, but progress was slow. In 1944, the Army ordered the integration of its training camp facilities. The Army Air Force began accepting black pilots. The 99th Fighter Squadron, a black unit from Alabama, was the first group of black pilots to see action during the war. Gradually, blacks began to be assigned combat roles and the all-black 761st Tank Battalion received a commendation for service in Germany. Even the Marines and Coast Guard began accepting African Americans.

The war years triggered a new black consciousness and militancy among African Americans, which led to the formation of the Congress of Racial Equality (CORE). This organization practiced nonviolent resistance such as sit-ins, marches, and demonstrations, techniques used frequently and effectively in the civil rights movement of the 1960s.

It wasn't until after the war, on July 26, 1948, that President Harry Truman officially ended all segregation in the armed forces. In general, World War II resulted in advancement in many areas for African Americans, but not the racial equality they believed was their right.

Hateful Voices of the People

The following excerpts focus on wartime attitudes toward the Japanese, their personal experiences within the internment camps, racism, and the treatment of African Americans.

(Source: *The Kikuchi Diary*, by John Modell. Urbana, Illinois: Board of Trustees of the University of Illinois Press, 1973, page 5)

...[The Japanese are] different in many respects...they are different in color; different in ideals; different in race; different in ambitions; different in their theory of political economy and government. They speak a different language; they worship a different God. They have not in common with the Caucasian a single trait...

— U.S. Webb
California Attorney General
Address to Congress, 1924

❖ ❖ ❖ ❖ ❖ ❖

(Source: Lingeman, *op. cit.*, page 336)

...Once a Jap, always a Jap...you cannot regenerate a Jap, convert him and make him the same as a white man any more than you can reverse the laws of nature...

— Congressman John Rankin
Congressional Record, December 15, 1941

❖ ❖ ❖ ❖ ❖ ❖

Government Poster

INSTRUCTIONS TO ALL PERSONS OF
JAPANESE
ANCESTRY

Pursuant to the provisions of Civilian Exclusion Order No. 33, this Headquarters, dated May 3, 1942, all persons of Japanese ancestry, both alien and non-alien, will be evacuated...by 12 o'clock noon...May 9, 1942.

No Japanese person...will be permitted to change residence after 12 o'clock noon...Sunday, May 3, 1942, without obtaining special permission from the representative of the Commanding General, Southern California Sector...

...The Following Instructions Must Be Observed:

1. A responsible member of each family, preferably the head of the family...will report to the Civil Control Station to receive further instructions...

2. Evacuees must carry with them on departure for the Assembly Center, the following property:

    (a) Bedding and linens (no mattress) for each member of the family;

    (b) Toilet articles for each member of the family;

    (c) Extra clothing for each member of the family;

    (d) Sufficient knives, forks, spoons, plates, bowls, and cups for each member of the family;

    (e) Essential personal effects for each member of the family.

All items carried will be securely packaged, tied and plainly marked with the name of the owner and numbered in accordance with instructions obtained at the Civil Control Station. The size and number of packages is limited to that which can be carried by the individual or family group...

❖ ❖ ❖ ❖ ❖ ❖

(Source: Satterfield, *op. cit.*, page 305)

I am for immediate removal of every Japanese on the West Coast to a point deep in the interior. I don't mean a nice part of the interior either. Herd 'em up, pack 'em off and give 'em the inside room in the badlands... Let 'em be pinched, hurt, hungry and dead up against it... If making one innocent Japanese uncomfortable would prevent one scheming Japanese from costing the life of one American boy, then let the million innocent suffer... Personally, I hate the Japanese. And that goes for all of them...

> — Henry McLemore
> Newspaper Columnist
> January 30, 1942

❖ ❖ ❖ ❖ ❖ ❖

(Source: *Beyond Words* by Deborah Gesensway and Mindy Roseman. Ithaca, New York: Cornell University Press, 1987, page 131)

It makes no difference whether the Japanese is theoretically a citizen. He is still a Japanese. Giving him a scrap of paper won't change him. A Jap's a Jap!

> — General John L. DeWitt
> Head of Western Defense Command
> Address to U.S. House of Representatives
> Naval Affairs Subcommittee
> April 13, 1943

The 10 Internment Camps for Japanese Evacuees

(Source: Rosenman, *1942 - Humanity on the Defensive, op. cit.*, page 177)

Name	Location	Capacity
Central Utah (Topaz)	West central Utah	10,000
Colorado River (Poston)		
Unit 1	Western Arizona	10,000
Unit 2	Western Arizona	5,000
Unit 3	Western Arizona	5,000
Gila River (Rivers)		
Butte Camp	Central Arizona	10,000
Canal Camp	Central Arizona	5,000
Granada (Amache)	Southeastern Colorado	8,000
Heart Mountain	Northwestern Wyoming	12,000
Jerome (Denson)	Southeastern Arkansas	10,000
Manzanar	East central California	10,000
Minidoka (Hunt)	South central Idaho	10,000
Rohwer	Southeastern Arkansas	10,000
Tule Lake (Newell)	North central California	16,000

Gallop Poll
1943

(Source: *For The Duration,* by Lee Kennett. New York: Charles Scribner's Sons, 1985, page 190)

Adjectives Americans most frequently used to describe Japanese:

barbaric	treacherous	bestial
evil	sneaky	sadistic
dirty	inhuman	savage

The Hirano family, left to right: George, Hisa, and Yasbei. Colorado River Relocation Center, Poston, AZ. Even Japanese Americans whose sons or husbands served in the U.S. military were not exempt. (WRA). National Archives.

In Response

Letter to President Franklin D. Roosevelt, April, 1943

Information that has come to me from several sources is to the effect that the situation in at least some of the Japanese internment camps is bad and is becoming worse rapidly. Native-born Japanese who first accepted with philosophical understanding the decision of their government to round up and take far inland all of the Japanese along the Pacific Coast, regardless of their degree of loyalty, have pretty generally been disappointed with the treatment that they have been accorded. Even the minimal plans that had been formulated and announced with respect to them have been disregarded in large measure, or at least, have not been carried out. The result has been the gradual turning of thousands of well-meaning and loyal Japanese into angry prisoners... [This] bodes no good for the future...

— Harold Ickes, Secretary of the Interior

These young evacuees of Japanese ancestry are awaiting their turn for baggage inspection upon arrival at this Assembly Center. Turlock, CA, May 2, 1942. Dorothea Lange. (WRA). National Archives.

❖ ❖ ❖ ❖ ❖ ❖

(Source: *Internees - War Relocation Center Memoirs and Diaries*, edited by Takeo Kaneshiro. New York: Vantage Press, 1976, pages 7-9)

...Japanese in Little Tokyo were ordered on May 2, 1942, to evacuate by May 9. It was so harsh an order that the Japanese had to do away with their merchandise and close their stores in one week. Some shopkeepers sold their goods by auction. They sold one pile of goods priced for so much, etc., and it was truly sorrowful. Those shopkeepers who did not place their goods on auction had an "Evacuation Sale," charging about ten cents for a load worth one dollar. In order to buy at the "Evacuation Sale" a crowd of Americans came to the Japanese section of town. This was perhaps the biggest crowd of people that ever congregated there...

...At last the departing day came: Friday, May 29, 1942. We were the last group of Japanese who were to leave the city of Los Angeles. I was full of deep emotion when I thought that from tomorrow there would be not even one Japanese walking in the greater Los Angeles area...

Roll call started at 6:00 A.M. We all got instructions and boarded the train... In each coach there were two U.S. soldiers on guard with rifles and bayonets... At 5:45 P.M. the train crossed the Colorado River and finally arrived at the station.

...Buses came... Finally, we arrived at the camp... My family registered and got Block 45-1-C. You may call it a room, but it had only a roof over it and it had only a floor. There were openings all around the walls and floor. It was no better than a beggar's hut. We had to make our own mattresses by filling bags with hay. Miserable indeed. I felt like crying...

— From the Diary of Kasen Noda

❖ ❖ ❖ ❖ ❖ ❖

June 8, 1942 Monday ...Although we are a drop in the bucket as far as numbers are concerned, the social implications and significance are of fundamental importance to this country as well as to the rest of the democratic world. How can we fight Fascism if we allow its doctrines to become a part of government policies? The contradiction would be too obvious to ignore...

— Diary of Charles Kikuchi

❖ ❖ ❖ ❖ ❖ ❖

I don't think you can actually tell people how awful it was at that time, how terrible it was. And how embarrassing, because we thought we were being such good citizens and everything. It was a terrible state to be in, really. It was awful. Yes it was. We didn't know what to do. We didn't know what was going to happen because the Japanese were winning at that time — all along. They were going into the Philippines and they were winning, you see. And I didn't want the Japanese to win. None of us did. We didn't want to be under Japanese rule, no...

— Lili Sasaki

❖ ❖ ❖ ❖ ❖ ❖

Some of the younger kids around town get angry at us because they say, "Why didn't you protest?" like people do now. They don't know what they're talking about. In those days, you just didn't do things that way. Actually we just didn't have the time; it was a shock and you didn't have the time to sit down and think about it. You just do what you're told and try to make the best of it.

I think we were forced into a situation and we weren't going to fight it. We just had to do the best we could in a bad situation.

— George Akimoto

❖ ❖ ❖ ❖ ❖ ❖

Manzanar

Poem by Michiko Mizumoto

(Source: Gesensway, Roseman, *ibid.,* page 108)

...They say your people are wanton
  Saboteurs.
  Haters of white men.
  Spies.

Yet I have seen them go forth to die for their only country,
Help with the defense of their homeland,
America.

I have seen them look with beautiful eyes at nature.
And know the pathos of their tearful laughter,
Chocked with enveloping mists of the dust storms,
Pant with the heat of sweat-days; still laughing.
  Exiles...

(Source: Bailey, *op. cit.,* page 149)

The Army jim crows [segregates] us. The Navy lets us serve only as messmen. The Red Cross refuses our blood. Employers and labor unions shut us out. Lynchings continue. We are disenfranchised [deprived of the right to vote], jim crowed and spat upon. What more could Hitler do than that?

— Unidentified Black College Student
Date Unknown

❖ ❖ ❖ ❖ ❖ ❖

Sign Carried By Black Man

Date Unknown

(Source: Harris, Mitchell, Schechter, *op. cit.*, page 97)

If Negro Men

Can Carry Guns for

Uncle Sam

Surely

They Can Drive Milk

Wagons For

Bowman Dairy

(Source: Harris, Mitchell, Schechter, *ibid.*, page 96)

...Blacks were extremely concerned over the fact that racism and bigotry and discrimination were a continuing practice in this country. Fascism was not a monopoly of Hitler, or of Mussolini, or the Japanese. It was something that we saw every day on the streets of Baltimore and in other places. We did not see much sense in the war unless it was tied to a commitment for change on the domestic scene. It made a mockery of wartime goals to fight overseas against fascism only to come back to the same kind of discrimination and racism here in this country...

— Alexander J. Allen

Growth, Prosperity, and Progress

by
Phyllis Raybin Emert

Although devastation, death, and brutality enveloped the globe from 1939 to 1945, the United States experienced staggering economic growth and prosperity on the home front in all areas during World War II.

More Americans were working, earning higher salaries, and spending more than ever before. Opportunity and optimism were in the air as the war began to wind down and new tax laws redistributed wealth in America. While the income of the richest fifth of the population increased by 20%, the income of the lowest fifth rose by 68%! This amounted to a doubling of the middle-class! Although the rich got richer, the quality of life for those on the lowest rung of the economic ladder also improved considerably.

The American worker, the businessman and the farmer all profited during the war years. The Federal government ballooned in size and supported technological advances in science and medicine which proved to be a benefit for all mankind.

In addition to developing weapons of war such as radar, rockets, explosives, and the atomic bomb, President Franklin D. Roosevelt's Office of Scientific Research and Development achieved great success in preserving and supporting human life. The development and mass production of the antibiotic, penicillin, along with improved sulfa drugs and dried blood plasma, helped prevent infection and kept alive most servicemen wounded in combat.

The manufacture and widespread use of the insecticide dichlorodiphenyltrichloroethane (DDT) killed lice and mosquitos which caused typhus and malaria among infantry soldiers in the field.

Other advances made by scientists during the war years included the use of radar for commercial airliners, jet-powered aircraft, air conditioning, new types of plastics, and the beginning of television and computer science.

The following table illustrates America's booming economic growth during World War II, comparing prewar and end of war statistics.

U.S. Growth Comparisons

(Compiled from statistics noted in Bailey, pages 145, 180-182; Ward, page 38; and *The Oxford Companion to World War II*, edited by I.C.B. Dear. Oxford, England and New York: Oxford University Press, 1995, page 1180)

Category	1939-1940	1945
Population	132 million	140 million
Federal Budget	$9 billion	$98.4 billion
Gross National Product (total production of goods and services)	$90 billion	$213 billion
Number of Americans who had to pay income taxes	7.8 million	48 million
College and University enrollment	1.4 million	1.7 million
Money spent on scientific research and development	$74 million	$1.6 billion
Federal employment	1 million	3.8 million
Labor Union membership	10.5 million	14.75 million
Population of the District of Columbia	900,000	1.3 million
Farm Income	$9.5 billion	$24 billion
Tractors	1.5 million	2.4 million
Weekly earnings of average factory worker	$25.25	$47.08
Percent of women in labor force	28.0	35.9
Percent unemployed	17.2	1.9

Aftermath of War

by
Phyllis Rabin Emert

Each and every American was affected by the Second World War in one way or another. The four years of U.S. involvement in this global conflict brought about financial and ideological changes in American society as well as political and personal ones.

Most major segments of the population were able to grow and prosper within the mainstream of American life during the war years because of the booming economy. Financial gains made by the poor, African Americans, and other minority groups improved their overall status in society and broke down many barriers to social and economic advancement. These advances brought a new-found confidence to blacks in particular, which led to an increased militancy in the civil rights movement that continued into the 1950s and 60s.

Many women earned money for the first time, and gained a self-esteem and confidence they had never before had. Women's self-image rose as they began to view themselves as independent and intelligent individuals who had the right to challenge or question male authority. Some women taught these new values to their daughters, guided them into colleges and careers, and encouraged them to make their own life choices in regard to marriage and the family. Many of these children (and their offspring) grew up and became early participants in the feminist movement of the late 60s.

Just as some whites resisted the movement for equality by African Americans, some men had difficulty with the new independence of postwar women. Servicemen often returned home to their wives only to find completely different women in their places. The pretty young things they left behind, who were more than happy to be home-makers and raise children, were no longer there. They had turned into strong-willed, practical and ambitious women who sampled a taste of the working world and discovered that they liked it and the freedom it offered.

Although many women returned to their former lives when the war ended, others wanted to continue working. The divorce rate skyrocketed. More than half a million couples split up in 1945 alone. The traditional role of the wife and mother was changing and many marriages simply couldn't survive the change.

The Second World War forever altered the role of the Federal government in America's social and political life. Along with big business, agriculture, and labor came big government, which took an active role in all aspects of American life as never before. Controversy surrounding the role of the federal government took the form of two opposing political ideologies. The conservatives (often Republicans) opposed this growing trend. They believed that all government was intrusive except at the local level, and had no place in the private lives of citizens. "The less government the better" was and still is their motto. The liberals (often Democrats) believed big government was the means by which the social and economic problems of society could be solved or lessened. To this day, American politics is shaped by these conservative and liberal viewpoints.

The United States emerged from the war an international super-power, the only country among the major participants whose home territory had not been touched by devastation or invasion. No longer able to continue its prewar isolationist policies, America was now a leader of world affairs, and maintained a large well-trained military force and defense system. With the development of atomic weapons, it became necessary for U.S. science and technology to keep a step ahead of the other major powers since the nation's security depended on it.

For many people, life after World War II became more complicated and stressful. Although things were simpler before Pearl Harbor, few Americans would have chosen to return to those days. In 1945 a victorious free nation, the richest, strongest and most productive in the world, faced life after the war with great hope and optimism.

The following excerpts focus on those who experienced living on the homefront and relate how the war changed their lives.

Life Will Never be the Same

(Source: Harris, Mitchell, Schechter, *op. cit.*, page 241)

Without the war I feel like I'd probably be back where I started from, working a few months a year, still struggling to make a living. So the war did bring on a better life as far as I was concerned. Working in the navy yard I gained a lot of skill in production. After the war I started building houses and used all that knowledge I had learned building ships. The building industry turned out very well for me. After all the hardships of the Depression, the war completely turned my life around.

— William Pefley

❖ ❖ ❖ ❖ ❖ ❖

(Source: Harris, Mitchell, Schechter, *ibid.*, pages 249-250)

Like a lot of women, I responded to the articles and the newspapers and the pressures from my family... I did what I thought was right. I went home. And I did all the things that I had been feeling guilty about not doing during the war. My husband would have been happy if I had gone back to the kind of girl I was when he married me — a little homebody there on the farm in the kitchen, straining the milk. But I wasn't that person anymore. I tried it for three years, but it just didn't work out. All at once I took a good look at myself, and I said no. No, you're just not going to do it. You're not going back where you started from. From here on in, you're your own person; you can do anything you want to. You're the same person you were in 1942. So I thought it was time then that we looked at ourselves, but my husband was satisfied. He was content to remain on the farm, but I wasn't. We argued constantly about it and became further and further apart. Finally, our marriage ended.

— Frankie Cooper

❖ ❖ ❖ ❖ ❖ ❖

(Source: Harris, Mitchell, Schechter, *ibid.*, pages 251-252)

Had it not been for the war I don't think blacks would be in the position they are now. The war and defense work gave black people opportunities to work on jobs they never had before. It gave them opportunity to do things they had never experienced before. They made more money and began to experience a different lifestyle. Their expectations changed. Money will do that. You could sense that they would no longer be satisfied with the way they had lived before...

I...saw in California that black women were working in many jobs that I had never seen in the South, not only defense work but working in nice hotels as waitresses, working in the post office, doing clerical work. So I realized that there were a lot of things women could do besides housework. I saw black people accepted in the school system and accepted in other kinds of jobs that they had not been accepted in before. It's too bad it took a war to motivate people to move here to want to make more of their lives...

— Sybil Lewis

❖ ❖ ❖ ❖ ❖ ❖

(Source: Satterfield, *op. cit.*, page 381)

...When we came back from Germany... I couldn't believe the changes. People weren't helping each other anymore. They were so busy with their own lives that they never went back to the old way of living before the war during the Depression. We suddenly got caught up in the hustle-bustle of a growing country with all its new technology learned in the war. We forgot about one another. We forgot about humanity...

— Florence Rudell Marx

❖ ❖ ❖ ❖ ❖ ❖

(Source: Harris, Mitchell, Schechter, *op. cit.*, page 236)

When the war was over we felt really good about ourselves. We had saved the world from an evil that was unspeakable... Good times were going to go on and on; everything was going to get better. It was just a wonderful happy ending.

— Laura Briggs

Bibliography and Suggested Further Reading

Bailey, Ronald H., Editor. *The Home Front: U.S.A.* Alexandria, Virginia: Time-Life Books, 1977.

Ehrlich, Gretel. *Heart Mountain.* New York: Penguin, 1989.

Gesensway, Deborah and Mindy Roseman. *Beyond Words.* Ithaca, New York: Cornell University Press, 1987.

Gluck, Sherna Berger. *Rosie the Riveter Revisited.* Boston: Twayne Publishers, 1987.

Goodwin, Doris Kearns. *No Ordinary Time.* New York: Simon & Schuster, 1994.

Greene, Bette. *Summer of My German Soldier.* New York: Bantam, 1984. Grades 7-12.

Hahn, Mary D. *Stepping on the Cracks.* Avon, New York, 1991. Grades 4-7.

Harris, Mark Jonathan, Franklin D. Mitchell and Steven J. Schechter. *The Home Front - America During World War II.* New York: G.P. Putnam's Sons, 1984.

Hoehling, A.A. *Home Front USA.* New York: Thomas Y. Crowell Company, 1966.

Houston, Jeanne W. and James D. *Farwell to Manzanar.* New York: Bantam, 1973.

Kaneshiro, Takeo, Editor. *Internees - War Relocation Center Memoirs and Diaries.* New York: Vantage Press, 1976.

Kennett, Lee. *For the Duration.* New York: Charles Scribner's Sons, 1985.

Kitagawa, Daisuke. *Issei and Nisei.* New York: The Seabury Press, 1967.

Leffland, Ella. *Rumors of Peace.* New York: Harper Perennial, 1985.

Modell, John, Editor. *The Kikuchi Diary.* Urbana, Illinois: Copyright Board of Trustees at the University of Illinois, 1973.

Piercy, Marge. *Gone to Soldiers.* New York: Fawcett, 1988.

Rosenman, Samuel I., Editor. *The Public Papers and Addresses of Franklin D. Roosevelt.* New York: Harper & Brothers Publishers, 1950.

Satterfield, Archie. *The Home Front.* New York: The Playboy Press, 1981.

Ward, Barbara McLean, Editor. *Produce and Conserve, Share and Play Square.* Portsmouth, New Hampshire: Strawberry Banke Museum and University Press of New England, 1994.

Weatherford, Doris. *American Women and World War II.* New York: Facts on File, 1990.